HEINEMANN STATE STUDIES

Uniquely Massachusetts

Carol Domblewski

Heinemann Library
Chicago, Illinois

Designed by Heinemann Library
Page layout by Heinemann Library
Printed in China by WKT Company Limited.

08 07 06 05 04
10 9 8 7 6 5 4 3 2 1

**Library of Congress
Cataloging-in-Publication Data**

Domblewski, Carol.
  Uniquely Massachusetts / Carol Domblewski.
    p. cm. -- (Heinemann state studies)
Includes bibliographical references (p.) and index.
  ISBN 1-4034-4470-6 (lib. bdg.) -- ISBN 1-4034-
4477-3 (pbk.)
  1. Massachusetts--Juvenile literature.
[1. Massachusetts.] I. Title.
II. Series.
  F64.3.D66 2004
  974.4'044--dc22

2003025716

Acknowledgments

The author and publishers are grateful to the
following for permission to reproduce copyright
material:

Cover photographs by (top, L-R) Kevin Fleming/
Corbis, Kevin Fleming/Corbis, Library of Congress,
Bruce Coleman, Inc.; (main) The Image Bank/
Getty Images

Title page (L-R) Burstein Collection/Corbis,
Geoffrey Clements/Corbis, Catherine Karnow/
Corbis; contents page, p. 15c Robert Dowling/
Corbis; pp. 4, 41 David Muench/Corbis; p. 5
Carolyn Lessard/AP Wide World Photo; p. 7 Bob
Krist/Corbis; p. 8 Chitose Suzuki/AP Wide World
Photo; p. 9 Alan Schein Photography/Corbis; p. 10
Robert Perron; p. 11 OneMileUp.com; p. 12b Ross
Frid/Visuals Unlimited; p. 12t Courtesy
Commonwealth of Massachusetts Art Commission;
p. 13b Dotte Larsen/Bruce Coleman, Inc.; p. 13t
Ned Therrien/Visuals Unlimited; p. 14 Joe
McDonald/Corbis; pp. 15b, 33 Catherine Karnow/
Corbis; p. 15t United States Department of the
Treasury; p. 16 North Wind Picture Archives;
pp. 17, 19 Burstein Collection/Corbis; p. 20 Todd
A. Gipstein/Corbis; pp. 22b, 23 Library of
Congress; p. 22t Steven Senne/AP Wide World
Photo; pp. 24, 30 Geoffrey Clements/Corbis; p. 25
Bettmann/Corbis; p. 26 Patricia McDonnell/AP
Wide World Photo; p. 27 PhotoDisc/Getty Images;
p. 29 Courtesy of Massachusetts Supreme Judicial
Court; p. 31 The Image Bank/Getty Images; p. 32
Jonathan Blair/Corbis; p. 34 Kelly-Mooney
Photography/Corbis; p. 35 Rolf Hansen Studio;
p. 36 The Granger Collection, New York; pp. 37,
44 Kevin Fleming/Corbis; p. 38b Reuters
NewMedia Inc./Corbis; p. 38t John Mottern/
AFP/Corbis; p. 39 Michael Dwyer/AP Wide World
Photo; p. 40 Lisa Poole/AP Wide World Photos;
p. 42 Lee Snider/Corbis; p. 43 Jon Hicks/Corbis

Photo research by Jill Birschbach

Special thanks to Professor Robert Allison of Suffolk
University for his expert comments in preparation
of this book.

Every effort has been made to contact copyright
holders of any material reproduced in this book.
Any omissions will be rectified in subsequent
printings if notice is given to the publisher.

Some words are shown in bold, **like this.**
You can find out what they mean by looking
in the glossary.

Contents

Uniquely Massachusetts

The word *unique* means different from all the rest. Among the 50 states, Massachusetts is unique in many ways. One way that Massachusetts is unique is its history. The state was a leader in three revolutions.

Many of the ideas and events that helped start the **American Revolution** (1775–1783) began in Massachusetts. It was the home of the **Boston Tea Party** and the birthplace of the **Sons of Liberty.** Massachusetts was also a leader in the **Industrial Revolution** (mid-1800s) in the United States. The state had the first large-scale factories to turn raw cotton into finished cloth. The state also helped lead the high-tech revolution. A scientist at the Massachusetts Institute of Technology (MIT) developed the first computer in 1925. The first e-mail was sent from a Massachusetts computer in 1971.

Just before the battles of Lexington and Concord on April 19, 1775, Captain John Parker gave his minutemen the instructions engraved on this stone.

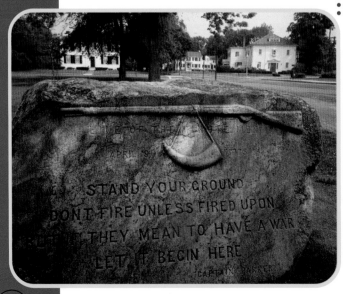

A Unique Name

The name *Massachusetts* is an Algonquian word. It is also the name of one of the state's Native American groups. The Massachusetts occupied the lands around what is now Boston and the Charles River when the first English settlers arrived in the 1600s. In

Algonquian, *massa* means "great" or "big," *chu* means "hill," and *et* is a **suffix** suggesting a place. Together, the word means "Great Hill Place."

MAJOR CITIES

Boston is the state capital. It is small in size and population for such a major U.S. city. It has about 600,000 people. It sits on 48 square miles, which makes it a fraction of the size of a city such as Dallas. Each weekday more than two million people come into the city by car, subway, train, plane, and boat. Boston Harbor is also the sixth busiest port on the Atlantic Ocean.

Founded in 1722, Worcester is the second largest city in the state and also in New England. Located in central Massachusetts, Worcester is one of just two U.S. cities to be named an All-America City a record five times, most recently in 2000. The All-America City Award is the highest community recognition award.

Springfield is the third largest city in Massachusetts. For many years, the Springfield **armory** fueled the economy of the city. Today, the city has a restored downtown, a lively Riverfront Park, and convention facilities. Tourists fill the Basketball Hall of Fame. They also visit the Armory complex, which is now a museum.

The ferry Alison *travels across Boston Harbor from East Boston to Long Wharf in downtown Boston.*

Geography and Climate of Massachusetts

Massachusetts has four major land regions, with plenty of variety—from rocky coasts to snowy mountains to tree-covered hills. The state also has a continental climate, which means that it has four distinct seasons.

COASTAL LOWLANDS

The Coastal Lowlands make up the eastern third of the state. The region includes Cape Cod and the islands of Nantucket and Martha's Vineyard. Cape Cod juts out into the Atlantic Ocean like a large arm. The region has hills, swamps, lakes, and short rivers. A major landform is the Great Blue Hills, south of Boston. They rise to a height of 635 feet. Several harbors also lie along the coast. They include Boston, Gloucester, and New Bedford.

English Place Names

Because it was once a British colony, many places in Massachusetts take their names from people and places in England. Among them are Boston, Cambridge, Worcester, Medford, Dorchester, Milton, and the Charles River.

CENTRAL MASSACHUSETTS

The Eastern New England Upland takes up the middle third of the state. The Upland is an extension of New Hampshire's White Mountains. The region rises to a height of about 1,000 feet and then gradually slopes downward toward the Connecticut Valley Lowland. Wachusett Mountain, at 2,006 feet above sea level, is the highest point in this region.

CONNECTICUT VALLEY LOWLAND

The Connecticut Valley Lowland is a long, slender region tucked next to the western edge of central Massachusetts. It extends from northern Massachusetts to southern Connecticut. In Massachusetts, the valley is twenty miles wide and is surrounded by hills in all directions except the south. The Connecticut River runs through the valley.

THE BERKSHIRES

The western part of Massachusetts is known generally as the Berkshires. However, the Berkshire Hills, an extension of Vermont's Green Mountains, are only in the northern part of this region. The land rises from the Connecticut Valley Lowland to heights of more than 2,000 feet. Mount Greylock, at 3,491 feet and the highest point in Massachusetts, is in this region.

Also in this region is a narrow path of lower land called the Berkshire Valley. It slices between the Berkshire and Taconic mountains, which are located on the western edge of the state. This valley is less than ten miles wide.

The western edge of the region features the Taconic Mountains. The Taconics slope from northwestern Massachusetts to the southwestern corner of the state. At 2,602 feet above sea level, Mount Everett is the highest point in this area.

The Berkshire Mountains surround Williams College in Williamstown, located in western Massachusetts.

Massachusetts Precipitation

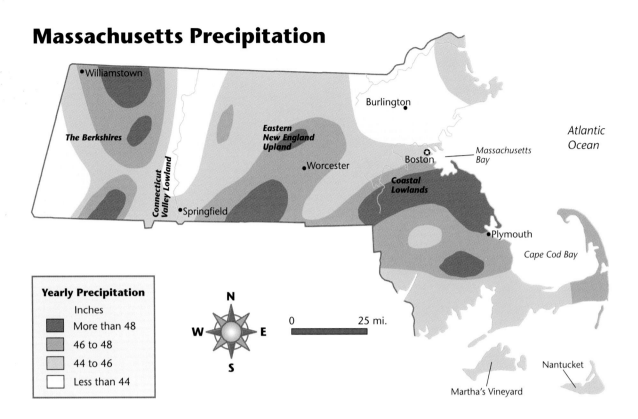

- •Williamstown
- The Berkshires
- Connecticut Valley Lowland
- Eastern New England Upland
- Burlington •
- •Worcester
- Boston ✪
- Massachusetts Bay
- Coastal Lowlands
- Atlantic Ocean
- •Springfield
- •Plymouth
- Cape Cod Bay
- Martha's Vineyard
- Nantucket

Yearly Precipitation

Inches

- More than 48
- 46 to 48
- 44 to 46
- Less than 44

N W E S

0   25 mi.

THE CLIMATE OF MASSACHUSETTS

Massachusetts has a continental climate. Summer temperatures in July average 72°F, while winter temperatures in January average 29°F.

The state's precipitation varies. The areas near the coast get about 43 inches per year, while the western mountains can receive as much as 75 inches per year. Occasionally, a blizzard called a **nor'easter** can blister the Massachusetts coast. It sweeps up the Atlantic coast and can drop several inches of snow. In 1995–1996, Boston received more than 100 inches of snow. That winter saw ten storms drop at least ten inches of snow around the city. One of the storms hit as late as the middle of April.

A nor'easter hammers Boston's Back Bay neighborhood during the winter of 2003.

Famous Firsts

EDUCATION FIRSTS

In 1635 the town of Boston founded the first public school in America, the Boston Latin School. It is the oldest public school in continuous existence in the country. From the earliest years, the town set aside public funds to support the school.

In 1636, Harvard College in Cambridge became the first college in the American colonies. The school was named for a minister, John Harvard, who left the college his books and half of his estate.

Established in 1848, the Boston Public Library was the first publicly supported city library in the country. It was also the first public library to lend a book, the first to have a branch library, and the first to have a children's room.

In 1870, the Boston Public Library (BPL) opened the first branch library in the United States in East Boston. The main BPL (left) has been at its present location in Copley Square since 1895.

TECHNOLOGY FIRSTS

In 1839 Charles Goodyear invented vulcanized rubber in Roxbury. The vulcanization process made the commercial use of rubber possible.

In 1845 Elias Howe, born in Spencer, invented the sewing machine in Boston. His invention helped revolutionize clothes manufacturing in factories and homes. Howe worked in cotton machinery factories in Lowell and Cambridge. He spent all his spare time trying to develop a practical sewing machine, and in 1846 he was granted a patent for it.

Boston's T rumbles through Brookline's Coolidge Corner. In the early 1900s, riding the T cost just five cents, and transfers were free.

In 1897 the nation's first subway system opened in Boston. It is known as the T.

In 1926 Robert Goddard, born in Worcester, launched the first successful liquid fuel rocket. In 1919 he wrote about the kind of rocket flight needed to reach the moon, a feat that would not be achieved for another 50 years. From his writing, he received enough research money to design and make the world's first rocket. Goddard attended Worcester Polytechnic Institute and Clark University in Worcester.

In 1950 Edmund Berkeley developed the first personal computer, Simon, in Boston. Personal computers capable of video output would not appear until the 1970s. Simon's communication consisted of a system of lights that lit up the front panel. Simon had a memory capacity of six small words. By 1959 plans for more than 400 had been sold.

Symbols of Massachusetts

STATE FLAG OF MASSACHUSETTS

The flag contains the state shield. In 1915, a pine tree was placed on the back of the flag. It stood for the importance of lumber in the early colonial economy. Currently, the flag contains the state **coat of arms** on one side only. The pine tree was removed.

The state adopted the final version of the flag in 1971.

STATE SEAL OF MASSACHUSETTS

The Massachusetts seal bears the coat of arms that appears on the state flag. In the middle of the shield stands an Algonquian person. The Algonquians and their ancestors were the first people to live in what is now Massachusetts. In the person's right hand is a bow. In the person's left hand is an arrow. The arrow points down to symbolize peace. Above the bow is a silver star with five points. The star represents Massachusetts as one of the original thirteen states. The Massachusetts seal says, *Sigillum Reipublicae Massachusettensis.* These Latin words mean "Seal of the Republic of Massachusetts."

The color blue on the shield is supposed to represent the Blue Hills of Canton and Milton, Massachusetts.

STATE MOTTO: *ENSE PETIT PLACIDAM SUB LIBERTATE QUIETEM*

Around the bottom of the shield that appears on both the seal and the flag are Latin words. They mean "By the sword we seek peace, but peace only under liberty." These words suggest that the people of Massachusetts would fight for peace, but only for a peaceful world in which people were free.

A five-foot-long cod, carved out of pine, hangs in the House of Representatives in the state capitol. Its head points to whichever party is currently in power.

STATE FISH: COD

To honor the importance of the sea and fishing in the state's economy, the cod became the official state fish in 1974. Cod is one of the state's most common fish. For the Pilgrims, Puritans, and many others, it also became an important money maker.

STATE FLOWER: MAYFLOWER

Made the state flower in 1918, the mayflower suggests the landing of the Pilgrims, because their ship was the *Mayflower.* A pink or white wildflower, the mayflower grows in woods and other shady places. It is also called a ground **laurel.** Since 1925 it has been on the **endangered** list.

The mayflower's evergreen leaves range from one to three inches long.

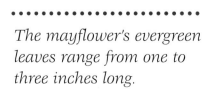

STATE TREE: AMERICAN ELM

The American elm became the official state tree in 1945. It was chosen because General George Washington took command of the Continental Army beneath an American elm on Cambridge Common in 1775. The **Sons of Liberty** are also said to have met under an American elm that they called the Liberty Tree. It is a large tree, with gray flaky bark. Its leaves turn yellow in the fall.

STATE MARINE MAMMAL: RIGHT WHALE

The right whale became a state symbol in 1980. Because whale oil was once a fuel for lighting, whaling brought in huge profits that helped build the state's economy. The right whale was large, slow, and likely to swim closer to shore than many other whales. As a result, it was hunted nearly to extinction. Today, however, the right whale is protected. It is slowly making a comeback.

The American elm can grow anywhere from 80 to 100 feet tall.

Because sailors made so much money from this whale between the 1600s and the 1800s, it earned the name right whale. *It was the "right whale" to catch.*

State Heroine: Deborah Sampson

Named the state heroine in 1983, Deborah Sampson fought in the **American Revolution.** She called herself Robert Shurtleff and dressed up as a man. No one knew she was a woman until she was wounded in battle. She received the first military **pension** ever given to a woman. May 23 is publicly remembered as the day she enlisted in the Continental Army.

State Game Bird: Wild Turkey

Wild turkey was probably eaten at the first Thanksgiving in America, which took place in Massachusetts. To honor this event and this important bird, the wild turkey became the state game bird in 1991.

Black-capped chickadees live in the northern two-thirds of the United States and much of Canada.

State Bird: Black-Capped Chickadee

The black-capped chickadee became the state bird in 1941. It is a happy-sounding bird that seems to call "chick-adee-dee-dee." One of the most familiar of the North American birds, it is only four to five inches long, and nearly half its length is in its tail!

Massachusetts State Quarter

Minted in 2000, the Massachusetts state quarter shows an outline map of the state. Crossing it is the full-length figure of a minuteman, musket in hand. The design honors the early soldiers

who played such an important role in the fight for independence from Britain. The quarter also says "The Bay State," which is a popular nickname for Massachusetts.

STATE DOG: BOSTON TERRIER

Adopted in 1979 as the state dog, the Boston terrier was bred in Boston. The Boston terrier is also sometimes called "the American gentleman among dogs" because of its gentle nature.

STATE BERRY: CRANBERRY

In 1994 Massachusetts adopted the cranberry as its state berry. In Massachusetts cranberries grow in **bogs.** Natural bogs evolved from deposits left by the glaciers more than 10,000 years ago. Massachusetts is second in the country in cranberry production.

The Boston terrier is loving and sensitive and has a deep love for its family and children.

Cranberries are one of three commercially grown fruits that are native to North America. Blueberries and Concord grapes are the other two.

Massachusetts History and People

The first people arrived in what is now Massachusetts from Asia thousands of years ago. The first people hunted, gathered, and fished. By 1500, several large groups of Native Americans lived in what would become Massachusetts. They were all Algonquians. Many groups spent summers by the coasts and winters inland. All these bands and groups spoke forms of the same language.

THE WAMPANOAG

One of the best-known Algonquian peoples are the Wampanoag. When Europeans first settled in America in the early 1600s, the Wampanoag homeland was in what is today southeastern Massachusetts and Rhode Island. At that time, the Wampanoag lived mainly by fishing, hunting, and farming. They hunted deer and other animals, which they used for both food and clothing. They also grew corn, squash, and beans.

THE FIRST EUROPEANS ARRIVE

When the Europeans first reached the coast of what would become Massachusetts around 1500, they needed fresh food and supplies. The

Algonquians are building one of their traditional dwellings, called a wigwam.

first Europeans had been on board ship for weeks or months. So the Europeans **bartered** with local Native Americans. In exchange for fresh food and other supplies, the Europeans sometimes gave the Native Americans tools and other metal items.

Europeans brought more than new goods. They also brought disease. Native Americans had never had diseases such as smallpox and measles before, so they could not fight them off. In some cases, whole groups were destroyed. In others, large numbers of people died all at once. Without even knowing it, the Europeans had begun to destroy native ways of life.

PILGRIMS AND PURITANS

Two main groups of English people settled in Massachusetts in the early 1600s. One was the Pilgrims. They left England to escape religious **persecution.** The Pilgrims arrived in 1620 on the *Mayflower.* First, they landed on what is today Cape Cod. Then they traveled to the place they named Plymouth.

The Pilgrims are remembered for many things. One is the first Thanksgiving. It followed their first harvest in 1621.

This painting from the 1800s presents an imaginary look at the Mayflower *coming ashore in Plymouth Harbor.*

The Pilgrims are also remembered for a document called the Mayflower Compact. The Pilgrims knew they needed some form of government in the new land. They agreed to join together to obey laws for the good of the whole community. Instead of following English laws, they

made their own laws. This was the beginning of self-government in America.

The second group of English people who settled Massachusetts was the Puritans. They were also hoping to practice their religion freely. John Winthrop led a large group of Puritans to North America in 1630. They founded Boston.

KING PHILIP'S WAR (1675–1676)

As tens of thousands of English people arrived, they farmed and fenced off more and more Native American land. The Native Americans finally decided they had to act, or they would lose all their land. A bloody war began in 1675. It was called King Philip's War. King Philip was the name that the English gave to a Wampanoag chief named Metacomet.

Losses were terrible for the settlers. At that time, there were 90 settlements in Rhode Island and Massachusetts. Native Americans attacked nearly half of them. They destroyed thirteen. Hundreds of settlers died in the war.

Losses were even more terrible for the Native Americans. They were defeated and captured. Some were killed. Some were sold into slavery. A whole way of life was changed forever. Estimates range from 500 to 3,000 killed.

GROWTH OF TOWNS AND CITIES

In 1691, the separate colonies of Plymouth and Massachusetts Bay joined together to form Massachusetts. By this time, trade by sea meant wealth for many. By the mid-1700s, the port cities of New Bedford, Newburyport,

Gloucester, Salem, and Boston were all bustling. Luxury goods from silver to silk found their way into the newly built mansions of successful sea captains and traders.

With the economy going strong, new communities were springing up all over. The population was growing. Between 1692 and 1765, the population rose to more than 222,000 people.

THE AMERICAN REVOLUTION

Until after the **French and Indian War** (1754–1763) ended, the colony got along fine with its mother country, England. The relationship was helpful to both sides. England protected the seas that the colonists used for trade. Colonists had many family and cultural ties to their mother country. Then England needed money for its wars in Europe and North America. It decided to tax the colonies. Taxes are payments made to support the government.

Crispus Attucks, who was killed during the Boston Massacre on March 5, 1770, was one of the first people to die for the cause of American independence.

People thought the taxes were unfair. They had no say in the decisions that were made in England. In Boston, a secret group called the **Sons of Liberty** formed. Samuel Adams was one of its leaders. Their slogan was "No taxation without **representation."**

Feelings against the British were strong. One day in 1770, a crowd in Boston began calling British soldiers names and acting as if they might hurt them. Scared, the British

soldiers fired into the crowd. Five deaths resulted, and the event became known as the Boston Massacre. Many colonists used the incident as a reason for disobeying British laws.

Then the Tea Act gave the British control over tea trade in the colonies. The colonists stood to lose a great deal of money as a result. In 1773, as an act of protest, colonists sneaked on board an English ship that was loaded with tea. They threw the tea into the harbor. This became known as the **Boston Tea Party.**

Signals from the Old North Church told Paul Revere whether the British were coming by land or by sea.

King George III of England punished the people of Boston with new laws. People called the laws "intolerable," which means they were too awful to accept. People decided they would rather fight than obey those laws. Militia, or groups of armed civilians, got ready to fight. In Massachusetts, this militia was called the minutemen. They were supposed to be ready to fight at a minute's warning.

THE FIGHTING BEGINS (1775)

If the British attacked first, messengers were ready to warn the colonists. One messenger was Paul Revere. Another was William Dawes. On the night of April 18, 1775, they warned the colonists that the British regular troops were coming.

The next day the battles of Lexington and Concord were fought. They were the first battles of the **American Revolution.** Because they had been warned, the Patriots—those against Britain—were ready. Though the British did some damage, they had to run back to Boston.

Although the war began in Massachusetts, it was soon fought in many colonies. By 1776, the colonies declared their independence from Britain. By 1783, the war was over, and the fight that had begun in Massachusetts was won. In 1788 Massachusetts became the sixth state to ratify, or pass, the U.S. **Constitution.**

THE INDUSTRIAL REVOLUTION

A different kind of revolution began in the United States in the early 1800s. Machines now did the work that was once done by hand. Also, many machines were in one place, not scattered in many places. In Massachusetts, the **Industrial Revolution** started in the cities of Waltham and Lowell. Lowell was the home of the first large-scale U.S. mill, or factory, to turn raw cotton into cloth. Mills meant jobs and goods. Jobs and goods meant money and trade. Money and trade led to the building of roads, canals, and railroads. People flocked to the mill towns. Some came from the farms to the cities. Others came from foreign countries.

In the 1840s, Ireland had a potato **famine.** Ireland had relied heavily on just the potato crop, and when it failed for several years, people began to starve. Because the British government did not help them, many Irish saw the United States as their best hope. Between 1846 and 1856, about two million Irish

The Lowell Girls

The mills changed people's lives. For the first time, women had jobs outside the home, farm, or schoolhouse. They left their homes and moved to the city. The first female factory workers in Lowell were called the Lowell Girls.

The 54th Massachusetts

The 54th Massachusetts was an all-black Civil War regiment. In 1863, it led an assault on Fort Wagner near Charleston, South Carolina. In the fight nearly half the unit was killed, wounded, or captured. For bravery in battle, William Carney became the first African American to earn the Medal of Honor, the nation's highest military award.

came to the United States. Hundreds of thousands settled in Massachusetts.

THE CIVIL WAR (1861–1865)

In the mid-1800s, Boston was home to many **abolitionists.** Massachusetts also had many stations on the **Underground Railroad.**

When the **Civil War** broke out in 1861, Massachusetts supplied the Union Army with guns, blankets, and tents. The city of Springfield made thousands of rifles. Shipyards in Massachusetts built many of the Union's ships.

Massachusetts supported the war in other ways, too. Nurse Clara Barton founded the American Red Cross, and Julia Ward Howe wrote "The Battle Hymn of the Republic." This song helped the Union troops find the courage and hope to keep going.

John Q. Adams

FAMOUS PEOPLE

John Adams (1735–1826), U.S. president. Born in Braintree, Adams helped lead Massachusetts and the colonies to declare independence from England. He served as the second president of the United States.

John Quincy Adams (1767–1848), U.S. president. Also born in Braintree, John Quincy Adams was the son of John Adams. In addition to being the sixth president, Adams was a diplomat, senator, and secretary of state.

Susan B. Anthony (1820–1906), reformer. Born in Adams, Anthony was an early leader in the fight for women's rights. She helped organize the woman **suffrage** movement.

Phillis Wheatley (1753–1784), poet. Born in present-day Senegal, Phillis Wheatley lived in Boston. She was the first African American to publish a book of poetry. Her first work was published in 1770.

Ralph Waldo Emerson (1803–1882), author. Born in Boston, Emerson was a great thinker who influenced many other writers. He wrote essays and poetry. He was also active in the antislavery movement.

Benjamin Franklin (1706–1790), statesman, inventor, author. Born in Boston, Franklin was a printer. He helped America become a new nation. He is also known for his many experiments and inventions. They include the lightning rod and **bifocals.**

Oliver Wendell Holmes (1809–1894), poet and essayist. Holmes was born in Boston. His most famous poems include "Old Ironsides" and "The Chambered Nautilus." Holmes was also **dean** of the Harvard Medical School.

Theodor Geisel (1904–1991), children's author. Born in Springfield, Geisel was better known as Dr. Seuss. He wrote funny, rhyming stories for children. They include the *Cat in the Hat* and *Green Eggs and Ham.*

John F. Kennedy

John F. Kennedy (1917–1963), U.S. president. Born in Brookline, Kennedy was the youngest person and first Catholic ever elected president. He served in the navy in **World War II** (1939–1945) and was a war hero. He was assassinated by Lee Harvey Oswald on November 22, 1963, in Dallas, Texas.

The American Revolution Begins

Massachusetts was home to many of the events that started the **American Revolution.**

PAUL REVERE'S RIDE

In April 1775, Paul Revere rode seventeen miles from Boston to Lexington and Concord to warn the colonial militia that the British troops were coming. According to the poem by Henry Wadsworth Longfellow, Revere waited for a signal flashed from the Old North Church in Boston before he took off. If it flashed once, the British troops were coming by land. If it flashed twice, they were coming by sea. The main message he and the others carried, however, was simply that the British troops were coming.

*Prior to his famous ride, Paul Revere also took part in the **Boston Tea Party** in 1773.*

LEXINGTON AND CONCORD

In April 1775, British General Thomas Gage learned about colonial military supplies stored outside Boston. He ordered his troops to Concord to seize these supplies. The British force of 700 men was met in Lexington by 77 local minutemen. They had been warned of the British raid by Paul Revere. However, colonial resistance melted away at Lexington. Then about 400 American patriots confronted the British at Concord's North Bridge and forced them to retreat. During the march back to Boston, the Americans fired on the British from behind trees and stone walls. This battle established **guerrilla** warfare as the colonists' way to fight the British.

BUNKER HILL

Two months after Lexington and Concord, the Battle of Bunker Hill took place on Breed's Hill in Charlestown. British soldiers tried to take the hill. They fought a bunch of farmers with few supplies. The colonial order "Don't fire until you see the whites of their eyes!" was given in order to save ammunition. The British won, but nearly half their soldiers were killed or wounded. During this battle, the British learned that the colonists had their hearts in the fight for independence.

This 1875 painting shows the American colonists and the British engaged in battle at the top of Breed's Hill.

Massachusetts State Government

The state government is run in the capital of Boston. Like the U.S. government, the government of Massachusetts is made up of three branches—the legislative branch, the executive branch, and the judicial branch. The Massachusetts **Constitution,** or plan for government, is actually older than the U.S. Constitution. Adopted in 1780, the Massachusetts Constitution is the oldest functioning written constitution in the world.

THE LEGISLATIVE BRANCH

The legislative branch is known as the General Court. It makes the laws. It is made up of two bodies like the ones in the U.S. Congress. One body is the Senate. It has 40 elected members. The other is the House of Representatives. It has 160 members. The General Court meets every year, but it does not meet all year long. Members of both the Senate and House of

Chief of Commerce and Labor Robert Pozen speaks during a legislative hearing on the state budget in 2003.

Representatives serve a term of two years and are limited to four terms.

Built in 1798, the capitol is located in Boston on top of Beacon Hill. The dome, originally made out of wood, is now made of copper and covered by 23-karat gold.

THE EXECUTIVE BRANCH

The governor is the most important person in the executive branch. There is also a lieutenant governor, who is a lot like a vice president. These leaders run the government day by day. They work closely with other members of the executive branch, including the governor's council. The governor's council includes the lieutenant governor and one member from each of eight state districts. There are also other officers such as a state treasurer and a secretary of state. Members of the executive branch are elected to their offices. They serve a term of four years and cannot serve more than two terms in a row.

The Massachusetts Supreme Court was established in 1692 and is the oldest appellate court in continuous existence in the Western Hemisphere.

THE JUDICIAL BRANCH

The judicial branch makes decisions based on the laws and applies the state's laws to real life situations. This branch of government is made up of different kinds of courts. The lowest courts include housing, juvenile, land, and **civil** courts. The Superior Court is the main trial court in the state. The Appeals Court handles all civil and **criminal appeals.** It has a chief justice and thirteen associate justices. The Supreme Judicial Court is the highest court of all. It can overturn decisions made by all the other courts in Massachusetts. All judges in Massachusetts are appointed by the governor. They can serve until the age of 70.

LOCAL GOVERNMENTS

Massachusetts is made up of fourteen counties. Each county has its own government. Commissioners and other officials, such as the sheriff and treasurer, are elected.

Each county contains many cities and towns. Each town or city can decide for itself what kind of government to

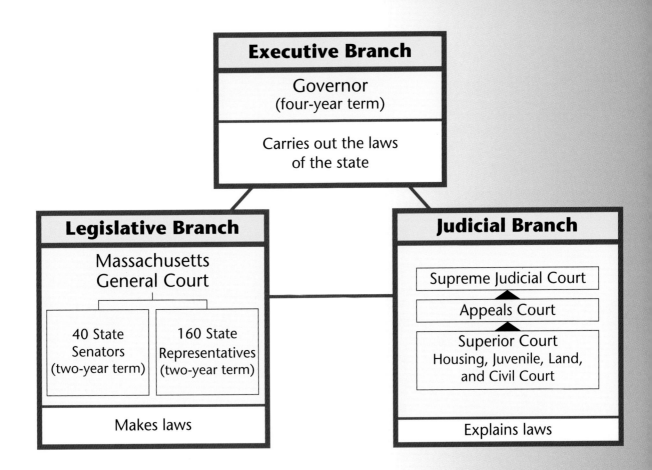

Executive Branch

Governor
(four-year term)

Carries out the laws
of the state

Legislative Branch

Massachusetts
General Court

| 40 State Senators (two-year term) | 160 State Representatives (two-year term) |

Makes laws

Judicial Branch

Supreme Judicial Court

Appeals Court

Superior Court
Housing, Juvenile, Land,
and Civil Court

Explains laws

choose. For example, Newburyport, which has about 20,000 people, is a city. Framingham, with approximately 70,000 people, calls itself a town.

Local governments vary. Cities are municipal governments. They are often made up of a mayor and a council. Sometimes they have a city manager and a council. Sometimes they are run by a group of people called commissioners.

Most towns are run by elected officials called selectmen. Many towns have a town meeting form of government. This is the most direct form of democracy in America. At a town meeting, every citizen can speak up about an issue and then vote on it.

Some towns have what is called a representative town meeting. In Burlington, for example, a few people are elected to represent all the townspeople. They speak up and vote at the town meeting.

Culture of Massachusetts

The culture of Massachusetts is rich and varied. The arts, education, music, and more thrive in the state.

Snap the Whip, *painted by Winslow Homer in 1872, shows children playing a game in a country setting.*

THE ARTS

Boston has been one of the U.S. cultural centers since before the **Civil War.** For example, it is home to the Museum of Fine Arts. This museum has some of the most beloved works in American painting. These include works by Massachusetts painters John Singleton Copley (1738–1815), Winslow Homer (1836–1910), and John Singer Sargent (1856–1925). For example, you can see Copley's famous painting of Paul Revere there. You can also see a characteristic Homer oil painting of a small boat being tossed about a frothy, green sea.

LEARNING IN MASSACHUSETTS

Education has been part of the culture of Massachusetts since the 1600s. The first American public secondary school was founded in Boston in 1635. The first free American public school was founded in Dorchester in 1639. Massachusetts was also home to the first board of education and the first school for the blind.

Some Massachusetts Colleges and Universities

Harvard University (1636) Cambridge; nation's first college

Williams College (1793) Williamstown; one of the nation's most competitive colleges

Amherst College (1821) Amherst; home to the first intercollegiate basketball game, 1859

Mt. Holyoke College (1837) South Hadley; first women's college in the country

Boston University (1839) Boston; first university to admit women on equal terms with men

College of the Holy Cross (1843) Worcester; one of the oldest U.S. Jesuit schools

Northeastern University (1844) Boston; had its beginnings as the first American community college

Tufts University (1852) Medford; only university in New England with a school of veterinary medicine

Massachusetts Institute of Technology (MIT) (1862) Cambridge; science and technology powerhouse with 56 Nobel Prize winners

Boston College (1863) Chestnut Hill; *U.S. News & World Report* ranks it among the top 40 national universities

Smith College (1871) Northampton; largest U.S. private college for women

Brandeis University (1948) Waltham; university named for Associate Justice Louis Brandeis, the first Jewish Supreme Court justice

Massachusetts is home to the Woods Hole Oceanographic Institute on Cape Cod. It is the largest independent center of ocean study in the world. Discoveries here have contributed to improving trade, health, national defense, and quality of life. Current research projects focus on plants and animals, global climate change, coastal erosion, and many other topics.

WESTERN MASSACHUSETTS

The western part of the state is also home to the arts. Tanglewood, located in Lenox, is the summer home of the Boston Symphony Orchestra. Jacob's Pillow, a dance center, was founded at almost the same time as Tanglewood. It stands where a station of the **Underground Railroad** once stood. The Pillow, as many call it, is more than a place to see dance. It is also a center for education and training in dance.

A group of musicians perform at Tanglewood, which was established in 1940.

Mass MoCA is a huge new museum in North Adams. It opened in 1999 and is the largest center for contemporary arts in the United States. It has more than 300,000 square feet of developed space. MoCA means Museum of Contemporary Art. There are 27 buildings on 13 acres devoted to the visual and performing arts. Old factory space now houses large works of art that could not fit in other buildings. These include paintings and sculptures that fill entire rooms.

Food of Massachusetts

Massachusetts is known for many kinds of food, but seafood is among the most popular.

SEAFOOD

When tourists visit the coast of Massachusetts, they often want lobster. Lobsters are served steamed, baked, and broiled. They are made into salads for lobster rolls. They also go into casseroles and other dishes.

Fried clams are a popular dinner all over the Massachusetts coast. Steamed clams, often served in buckets, find their way onto hundreds of menus. Clams are also the main ingredient in New England clam chowder. This Massachusetts standby is a white, milky soup. It usually contains potatoes and onions.

No Love for Lobster

Today, many people love lobster. A common size for a lobster is a more than one pound. The Pilgrims pulled lobsters that weighed up to twenty pounds out of the water. They were not thrilled by that, however. The Pilgrims ate lobster only when there was nothing better to eat. The Puritans served it to prisoners, servants, and the poor. Native Americans used the meat for fish bait.

Cooks prepare clams and lobster for a clambake on Martha's Vineyard.

The clambake is a New England tradition. The Wampanoag probably invented it. They still bake clams, other shellfish, and vegetables over hot rocks. The food is covered with seaweed to prevent burning and to salt the food.

BEANTOWN

Baked beans have been a traditional dish since colonial days. Beans were served so often that Boston became known as Beantown. Massachusetts even has a state bean—the navy bean.

Chocolate Chip Cookies

(the official Massachusetts state cookie)

1 cup butter	2 1/4 cups all-purpose flour
3/4 cup sugar	1 teaspoon baking soda
3/4 cup brown sugar	3/4 teaspoon salt
2 eggs	2 cups chocolate chips
1 teaspoon vanilla extract	

Have an adult help you with the electric mixer and the oven.

1. Preheat oven to 350° F and lightly grease two cookie sheets.
2. In a large bowl, cream together the butter, brown sugar, and white sugar until light and fluffy.
3. Beat in the eggs one at a time and stir in the vanilla.
4. Mix the flour, baking soda, and salt together and stir this mixture into the creamed mixture. Then stir in the chocolate chips.
5. Drop rounded spoonfuls onto the cookie sheets.
6. Bake eight to ten minutes. Cookies should be lightly browned and still a little soft to the touch. Allow cookies to cool for a few minutes.

Massachusetts Folklore and Legends

People have always passed along their folk tales. Some tales entertain, and others teach history. Most do a bit of both.

The Return of Chief Greylock

Chief Greylock lived in the Waranoke village, which is now the town of Westfield. His native name was Wawamolewat. He saw many changes in his lifetime. At first his people were friendly with the British. But, over time, Wawamolewat's lands and the animals his people hunted disappeared. This caused the tribe to move to the Berkshires. Chief Greylock had a secret cave on the slope of Mount Greylock. There he caused as much trouble as he could for the settlers.

Now, legend has it, he is back. In 1901, there was a landslide on Mount Greylock. The tumble of rock it left became known as the Chief's Steps. Then in 1990, tons of rocks crashed down the side of the

This bare spot on the side of Mt. Greylock is supposedly the face of Wawamolewat himself.

mountain. On May 14, a giant face seemed to appear in the mountain, looking straight at the people of Adams. Some people say it is Greylock himself.

THE CURSE OF THE BAMBINO

The Bambino is Babe Ruth. Early in his career he played for the Boston Red Sox. In 1920 Boston sold him to the New York Yankees for $125,000. Since then, the Boston Red Sox have never won another World Series. Red Sox fans call this run of bad luck the Curse of the Bambino.

OVER THE RIVER AND THROUGH THE WOODS

People throughout the country sing a song with the lines "over the river and through the woods, to grandmother's house we go." However, few know where the song comes from. A woman from Medford wrote the words in 1844. The river referred to is the Mystic. The author, Lydia Mariah Child, an **abolitionist,** was on her way to her grandfather's house when she wrote the story.

In the late 1800s, a company called Currier and Ives made more than 7,000 lithographs. They provided views of American life, including this one of a horse-drawn sleigh.

Massachusetts Sports

Massachusetts is home to many professional sports, including basketball, baseball, football, and hockey.

BASKETBALL

Basketball was invented in Springfield by James Naismith. The first basketball game was played there in 1891. The city is the home to the Naismith Memorial Basketball Hall of Fame, which opened in 1968.

The Boston Celtics have won sixteen National Basketball Association (NBA) championships. Celtic greats include Larry Bird, Bill Russell, and Kevin McHale. Celtic Paul Pierce leads the team today. The Celtics play their games at the Fleet Center.

BASEBALL

The Boston Red Sox have played in Fenway Park since 1912. Fenway is the oldest major-league ballpark in the

One of the unique features of Fenway Park is its 37-foot-high leftfield fence, called the Green Monster for its size.

Patriots' quarterback Tom Brady throws a pass downfield in the fourth quarter of the 2002 Super Bowl.

country. Famous players for the Red Sox have included Carl Yastrzemski, Ted Williams, and Roger Clemens. Current stars include Nomar Garciaparra and Pedro Martinez.

FOOTBALL

The New England Patriots made football history when they won Super Bowl XXXVI in 2002. Led by quarterback Tom Brady, the Patriots drove down the field in the final seconds to set up a game-winning field goal. The Patriots play their home games at Gillette Stadium in Foxborough.

HOCKEY

The Boston Bruins have won five National Hockey League (NHL) Stanley Cup Championships. Bobby Orr and Ray Bourque are among their greatest players ever. The Bruins set an NHL record by making the playoffs 29 straight years between 1967 and 1996. The Bruins, like the Celtics, play at the Fleet Center.

THE BOSTON MARATHON

A marathon is a 26-mile footrace. The Boston Marathon was first run in 1897 and is the oldest marathon in the country. It begins in the suburb of Hopkinton and ends in downtown Boston.

Marathoners take off on their 26-mile trek in the 2003 Boston Marathon.

Businesses and Products of Massachusetts

Today, Massachusetts still leads the way in many areas. These include biotechnology, high technology, medical care, and medical research.

MANUFACTURING

Massachusetts has some of the largest manufacturing and technology companies in the country. For example,

The Big Dig

A famous solution to traffic problems in Boston was the Big Dig. Workers moved the Central Artery, a major highway, below ground. What is so big about the Big Dig?

- Workers dug up sixteen million cubic yards of dirt. That is enough to fill up a major sports stadium about fifteen times.
- Workers moved 29 miles of gas, electric, telephone, sewer, water, and other utility lines.
- Workers poured more than 3.8 million cubic yards of concrete. That is enough to build a sidewalk from the Atlantic Ocean to the Pacific Ocean and back again three times.
- The plan created more than 150 acres of parks.

the Gillette Company, founded in 1901 when King C. Gillette invented the safety razor, is headquartered in Boston. Gillette has thousands of employees and has manufacturing plants all over the world. It not only makes shaving products but Duracell batteries, Braun electronics, and Oral-B products as well.

TECHNOLOGY

Massachusetts is home to the biotechnology industry. Biotechnology uses information in **genes** to develop new products and cures. Genzyme, a biotechnology company headquartered in Cambridge, has been in business since the early 1980s. Among the many products they have produced is Carticel®. Introduced in 1997, it is designed to repair **cartilage** in the knee—a first for a cell therapy product.

A fisher in Gloucester sorts a catch of cod and pollack. The Sarah-Kate brought in nearly 10,000 pounds of fish on a two-day trip in 2002.

Massachusetts also has many high technology companies. For example, Raytheon, headquartered in Waltham, is a defense technology company. Begun in 1922, Raytheon helped improve the production of radar during **World War II** (1939–1945). During the **Persian Gulf War** (1991), Raytheon's Patriot Missile intercepted Iraqi missiles fired at Israel and Saudi Arabia. The Patriot became the first missile ever to intercept an enemy missile in combat.

FISHING

With an annual catch valued at more than $280 million, Massachusetts ranks in the top five in fishing in the country. The town of New Bedford accounts for nearly half of the scallops gathered in the United States.

Attractions and Landmarks

Massachusetts draws tourists from all over the world for its history, scenic beauty, and culture.

THE FREEDOM TRAIL

The 2.5-mile trail begins at the Boston Common and ends at the Bunker Hill Monument. Along the trail, visitors can see the site of the Boston Massacre, which took place in front of the Old State House. They can visit the Old South Meeting House, where revolutionary ideas were discussed. The trail also includes Paul Revere's house, as well as the Old North Church where the two lanterns were hung just before his ride.

The Granary Burial Ground is also on the Freedom Trail. Buried here are some of the greatest leaders of the **American Revolution,** including John Hancock and Paul Revere.

BLACK HERITAGE TRAIL

This Boston walking trail is a little more than 1.5 miles long. It includes the Charles Street Meeting House. In this building, both Frederick Douglass and Sojourner Truth

Bunker Hill Monument opened in 1842. The 221-foot granite tower marks the site of the first major battle of the American Revolution.

spoke out against the evils of **slavery.** The trail also includes stops along the **Underground Railroad** and the monument to the 54th Massachusetts Regiment.

PLIMOTH PLANTATION

Plimoth Plantation in Plymouth recreates life at the time of the Pilgrims in the 1600s. Visitors can learn about the settlers' homes, gardens, fields, dress, furniture, and more. Wampanoag ways of life are also recreated. They include the homes, arts and crafts, clothing, and tools of the Wampanoag at the time of the Pilgrims.

FANEUIL HALL

Another building in Boston is Faneuil Hall. Peter Faneuil was once Boston's richest merchant. He built Faneuil Hall in 1742 as a public market and meeting place for the people of Boston. Many discussions about the **American Revolution** took place there.

Today, next to Faneuil Hall is the Faneuil Hall/Quincy Marketplace, which houses a food court.

LOWELL NATIONAL HISTORIC PARK

The purpose of Lowell National Historic Park is to help visitors understand life in Lowell at the time of the mills in the 1800s. Visitors can see how the power of the Merrimack River was used to produce and transport cloth. They can also visit recreations of the mills themselves, as well as places where workers lived, worshiped, and gathered.

MINUTEMAN NATIONAL HISTORIC PARK

At Minuteman National Historic Park, visitors can see sites and learn about Paul Revere's ride, as well as the fighting that took place during the battles of Lexington and

Places to See in Massachusetts

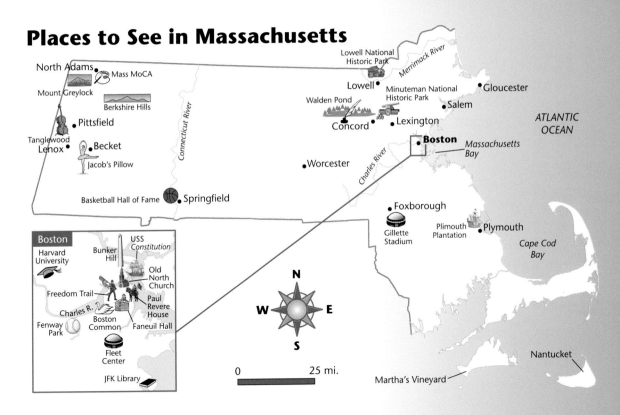

Concord. The routes of the minutemen who fought on April 19, 1775, are traced. The Concord Monument marks the place where the Patriots fired "the shot heard round the world."

THE JOHN F. KENNEDY LIBRARY

The library is a museum and a research center. It is also a memorial to the 35th president. It opened to the public in 1979. This dramatic modern building sits on the harbor south of the city of Boston. Inside, visitors can see films, listen to speeches, and view items from the lives of the president and his family.

CAPE COD NATIONAL SEASHORE

In 1961, Congress created the Cape Cod National Seashore. It is a strip of seashore 40 miles long. For almost half a century, it has provided a home for wildlife. Besides swimming and

Built in 1872, the Wood End lighthouse sits at the entrance to the Provincetown Harbor.

The U.S.S. Constitution *was built between 1794 and 1797 and still holds an honorary commission in the U.S. Navy.*

sunbathing, the area also offers hiking, biking, and other pastimes.

U.S.S. CONSTITUTION

The U.S.S. *Constitution* is the oldest commissioned warship in the world, and its crew are active duty sailors in the U.S. Navy. The ship is docked in Charlestown Navy Yard. With the nickname of "Old Ironsides," the ship was first used in the **War of 1812** when repeated shots failed to sink it. It won 33 fights at sea.

WALDEN POND

In Concord lies one of the most famous bodies of water in the United States. Actually a lake, Walden Pond was the site of Henry David Thoreau's (1817–1862) two-year experiment of living in the woods. The book *Walden* was the result. Today, visitors swim, fish, picnic, and hike there. They also visit the site of Thoreau's cabin.

Map of Massachusetts

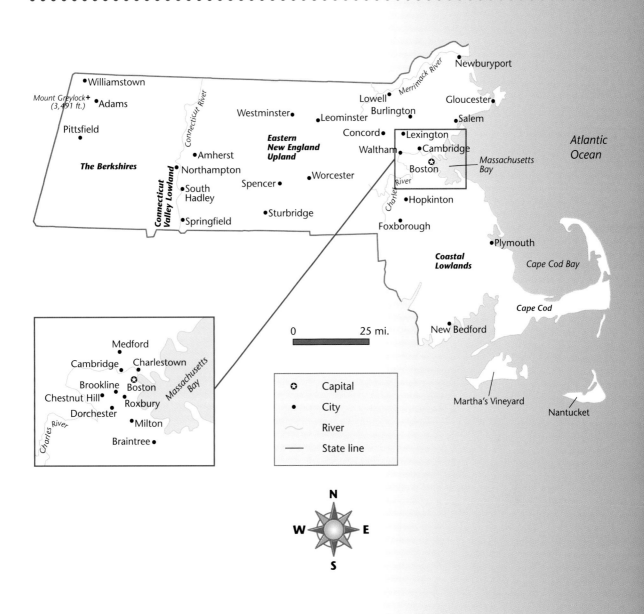

Williamstown

Mount Greylock+
(3,491 ft.)   Adams

Pittsfield

The Berkshires

Newburyport

Merrimack River

Lowell

Burlington

Gloucester

Westminster   Leominster   Salem

**Eastern
New England
Upland**

Concord   Lexington

Waltham   Cambridge

*Massachusetts
Bay*

Amherst   Boston

Northampton   Charles River

South
Hadley   Spencer   Worcester   Hopkinton

**Connecticut
Valley Lowland**

Springfield   Sturbridge   Foxborough

*Atlantic
Ocean*

**Coastal
Lowlands**   Plymouth

Cape Cod Bay

Cape Cod

New Bedford

Connecticut River

0   25 mi.

Medford

Cambridge   Charlestown

Brookline   Boston

Chestnut Hill   Roxbury   *Massachusetts Bay*

Dorchester

Milton

Charles River

Braintree

☼   Capital
•   City
∿   River
—   State line

Martha's Vineyard

Nantucket

N
W   E
S

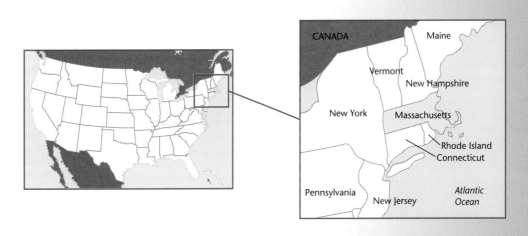

CANADA   Maine

Vermont

New Hampshire

New York   Massachusetts

Rhode Island
Connecticut

Pennsylvania

New Jersey   *Atlantic
Ocean*

Glossary

abolitionists people who wanted to end slavery forever

American Revolution between 1775 and 1783, the war for American independence between American colonists and Great Britain

appeal to transfer a legal decision from a lower court to a higher court for a review of the lower court's legal decision

armory place where weapons are stored

barter exchange or trade of goods without money

bifocals glasses in which one part corrects near vision and another part corrects vision for distance

bog wet, spongy ground

Boston Tea Party raid by American colonists on three ships in Boston Harbor on December 16, 1773. Colonists disguised as Native Americans emptied 342 chests of tea into the harbor to protest a British tax on tea.

cartilage substance that serves as a protective layer where bones come together

civil having to do with private citizens

Civil War from 1861 to 1865, a war between the Southern states, trying to preserve slavery and a farming way of life, and the Northern states, wanting a more modern way of life and to end slavery

coat of arms collection of symbols that represent a family, country, or other group

constitution document that defines and explains governments

criminal having to do with a crime

dean leader or director

endangered at risk of dying out

famine a food shortage over a long period of time

French and Indian War from 1754 to 1763, it was fought mainly between France and Britain. The war resulted in Britain gaining almost all of France's territory in North America.

gene cell that determines which characteristics living things get from their parents

guerrilla method of fighting by using small, surprise attacks

Industrial Revolution during the late 1700s and early 1800s, the introduction of power-driven machinery and the development of factories that changed the lives and work of people in several parts of Europe and North America

laurel type of evergreen plant

nor'easter storm with strong northeasterly winds that results from a low pressure system along the Atlantic coast and causes large waves, storms, and beach erosion

pension set amount paid regularly to a person

persecution to cause to suffer because of a belief

Persian Gulf War in 1991, fought between Iraq and 39 countries organized mainly by the United States and the United Nations (UN). The war took place in Iraq and Kuwait.

representation elected person representing a group's political interests

slavery practice in which people own other people. During the 1500s and 1600s, the colonization of the Americas by Europeans resulted in an expansion of slavery.

Sons of Liberty group of patriotic societies that sprang up before the American Revolution

suffix a word ending

suffrage right to vote

War of 1812 fought between the United States and Great Britain over English interference in American shipping

World War II between 1939 and 1945, fought between the Axis powers (Germany, Japan, and Italy) and the Allies (United States, Soviet Union, and Great Britain)

Underground Railroad secret network that helped African American slaves escape to freedom in the North or Canada

More Books to Read

Bjorklund, Ruth. *Massachusetts.* New York City: Benchmark Books, 2003.

Hodgkins, Fran. *Massachusetts.* Mankato, Minn.: Capstone Press, 2003.

LeVert, Suzanne. *Massachusetts.* New York City: Marshall Cavendish, 2000.

McNair, Sylvia. *Massachusetts.* Danbury, Conn.: Children's Press, 1998.

Index

About the Author

Carol Domblewski has been writing and editing educational materials for more than 25 years. She is proud to live in Acton, Massachusetts, where she loves everything but the weather.